The Dandelion Friends Series

The Dandelion Friends and the Gentle Garden Gathering

Gentle Poses for Brave Little Hearts

Created with love by
Lisa Bolton

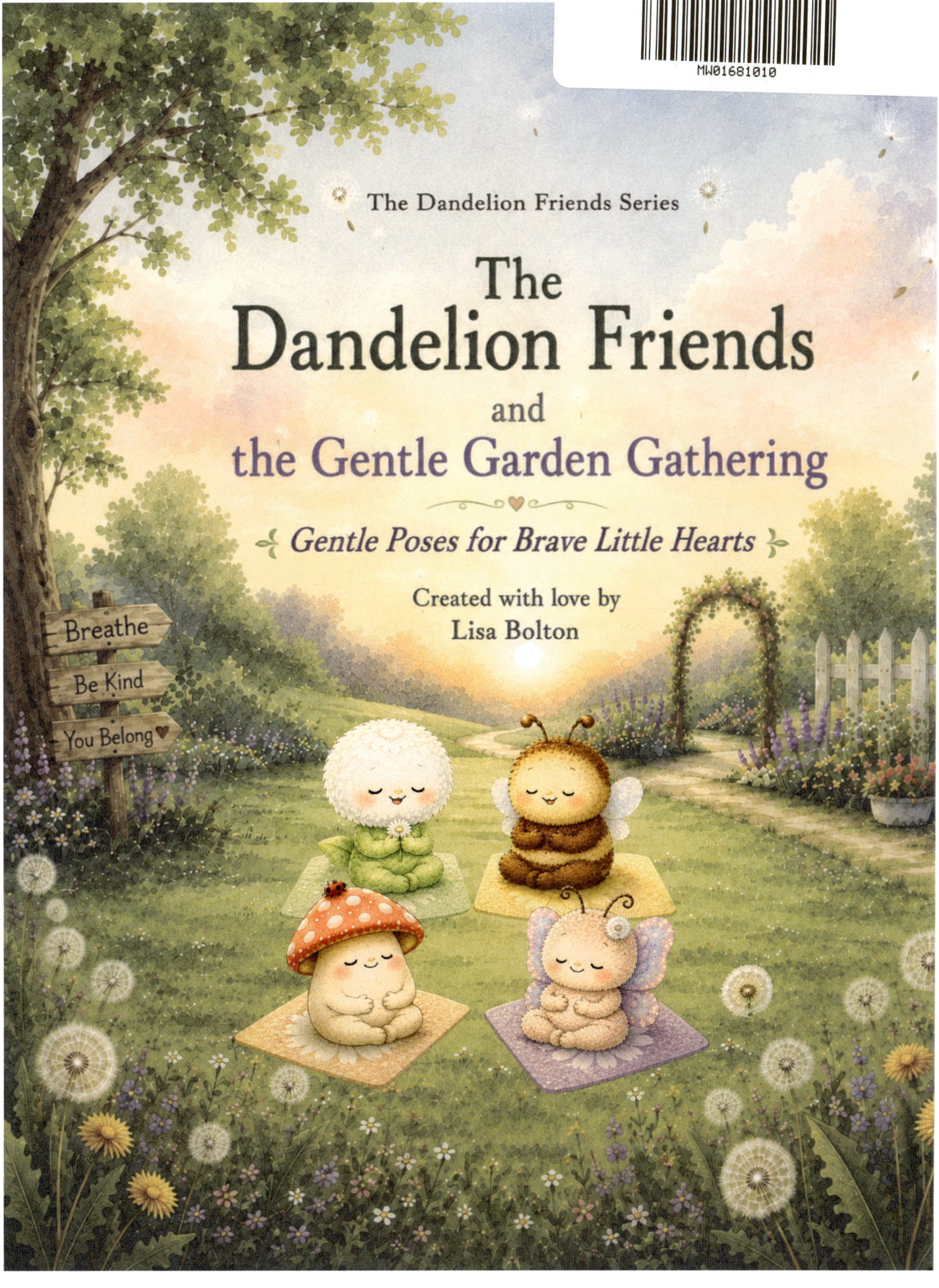

Written and created with love by Lisa Bolton
Illustrations created for The Dandelion Friends Series

First Edition

ISBN: (Paperback) 979-8-9951462-8-5

Published by The Dandelion Project
Ocala, Florida
dandelionproject.net

Printed in the United States of America

The Dandelion Friends
Gentle Poses for Brave Little Hearts
Featuring:
Kerri the Dandelion
Quinn the Mushroom
DJ the Bumblebee
Betty the Butterfly

Welcome, Brave Little Heart
This book was created to be a soft place to land.
Inside these pages, you'll meet Kerri and her friends —
gentle guides who help children move, breathe,
and feel safe in their bodies.
These poses are not about being perfect.
They are about feeling calm, strong, and loved.
Take your time.
Breathe slowly.
And remember —
you are never alone on your journey.

For Kerri —
whose love of yoga and peaceful movement
taught us that calm lives inside every breath.
And dedicated to my children —
Kerri, DJ, and Quinn.
Your love planted the seeds for this work
and continues to grow hope and comfort
for children and families everywhere.
May every child who opens this book
feel safe, peaceful,
and surrounded by love that never leaves

Meet the Friends of the Garden

In the Garden of H.O.P.E, gentle friends help each other move, breathe, and grow. Each friend has something special to share.

Kerri the Dandelion
Kerri loves peaceful mornings in the garden. She discovered that yoga helps her feel calm, balanced, and strong.

DJ the Bumblebee
DJ reminds us that even the smallest light can shine brightly. He teaches us how to stand tall and be brave.

Quinn the Mushroom
Quinn knows that quiet moments can make us feel safe and peaceful. She shows us how to slow down and rest.

Betty the Butterfly
Betty teaches us that movement can be gentle and joyful. Her wings remind us that change can be beautiful.

Together, they help the garden grow with calm, strength, and friendship.

Kerri loved to move her body in gentle,
peaceful ways.
Yoga helped her feel calm inside —
like her heart could take a deep breath.
Now, she shares that calm with you.
Together with her friends —
DJ, Quinn, and Betty —
she invites you to stretch, breathe,
and grow brave.
There is no rush.
No right or wrong.
Just follow along...
one gentle pose at a time.
Are you ready?
Let's begin.

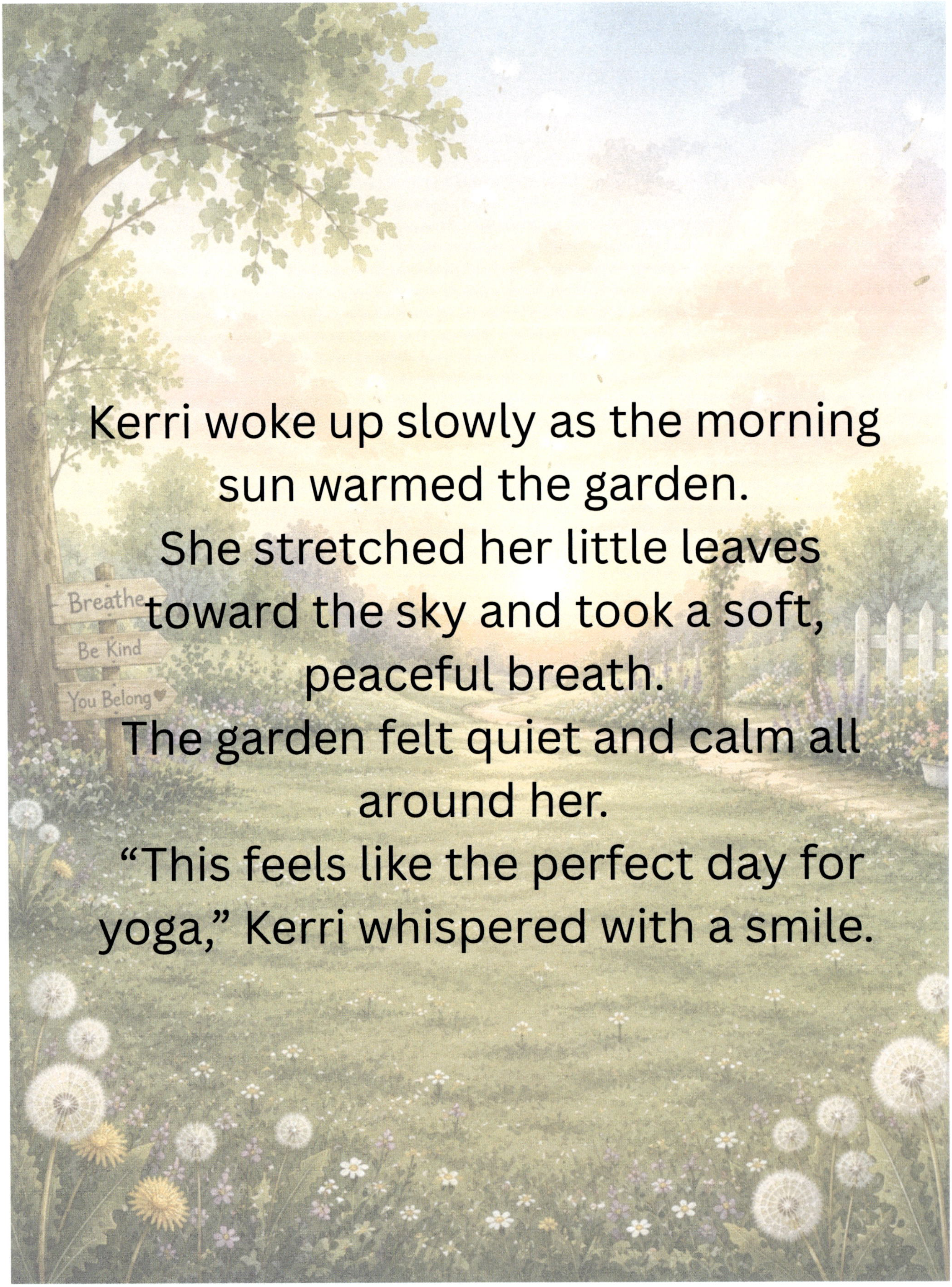

Kerri woke up slowly as the morning sun warmed the garden.
She stretched her little leaves toward the sky and took a soft, peaceful breath.
The garden felt quiet and calm all around her.
“This feels like the perfect day for yoga,” Kerri whispered with a smile.

Kerri and DJ followed the winding garden path together.

Along the way, they invited Betty and Quinn to join them. “Come with us,” called Kerri. “We're going to spend the morning stretching, breathing, and having fun together!”

The friends sat together in the soft morning grass.
Kerri smiled gently at each of them.
"Yoga helps our bodies stretch and our hearts feel calm," she explained.
"We don't have to be perfect. We just breathe, move, and try our best together."

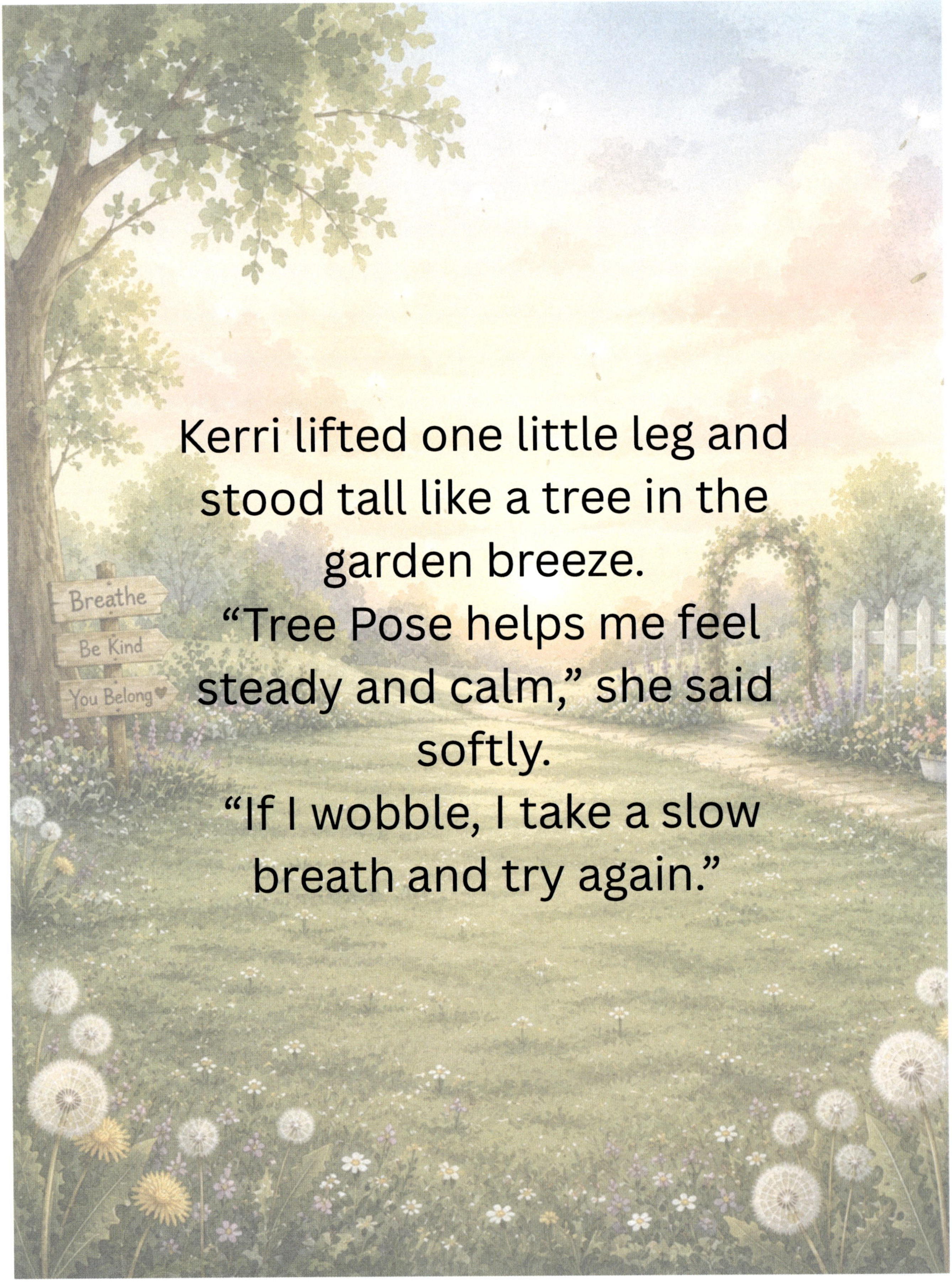

Kerri lifted one little leg and stood tall like a tree in the garden breeze.
"Tree Pose helps me feel steady and calm," she said softly.
"If I wobble, I take a slow breath and try again."

Affirmation:
"I stand tall and strong."
Breathe
Be Kind
You Belong
Tree Pose

DJ stood tall and still on his fuzzy little feet.
He took a deep breath and lifted his head proudly.
“Mountain Pose helps me feel strong and steady,” DJ buzzed happily.

Affirmation:
"I stand tall, calm, and full of peace."

Mountain Pose

Quinn stood up bravely and placed her hands on her hips.

“Hero Pose reminds me that being calm can also be brave,” she whispered gently.

Hero Pose

Affirmation:
"I am brave, kind,
and full of courage."

Betty sat peacefully in the warm garden sunlight.
"Lotus Pose helps me slow down and listen to quiet thoughts," she said with a smile.

Lotus Pose

Affirmation:
"I am calm, peaceful,
and full of light
inside and out."

Kerri crossed her little legs, and closed her eyes for a moment. "Easy Pose is a wonderful time for breathing slowly," she explained.

"Slow breaths help my whole body relax."

Affirmation:
"Peace begins inside me"
Breathe
Be Kind
You Belong
Easy Pose

DJ took a deep breath and
stretched his fuzzy arms wide.
“Warrior Pose helps me feel
brave and strong,” he said.
“When my thoughts start buzzing
too fast, I stand tall and breathe
slowly.”

Affirmation:
"I am brave, strong, and ready to shine."
Breathe
Be Kind
You Belong
Warrior Pose

Quinn curled up carefully beneath her mushroom cap and rested quietly on the grass.
"Child's Pose helps me feel safe and peaceful," she whispered softly.

Affirmation:

"I am safe, calm,
and loved just as I am. ."

Child Pose

Betty fluttered her wings
gently as she moved her legs
up and down.
“Butterfly Pose makes me feel
light and happy,” she giggled.
“Like I’m floating on a soft
garden breeze.”

Affirmation:

"I open my heart, stretch my wings, and gently grow stronger every day."

Butterfly Pose

The friends stretched their arms and legs out wide together. “Star Pose reminds us that every friend can shine in their own special way,” Kerri said proudly.

Affirmation:

"I shine bright, strong, and calm just like the stars above the garden."

Star Pose

The friends sat together
in a peaceful garden
circle.
They breathed slowly,
smiled gently, and
enjoyed the quiet
moment together.

Affirmation:

"I breathe in peace
and blow out my worries
like dandelion seeds."

Garden Circle Pose

The garden grew calm and quiet as the friends rested together beneath the glowing sky.

Soft breezes drifted through the flowers while everyone breathed slowly and peacefully.

Affirmation:

"Rest helps my body,
heart, and mind grow
peaceful and strong."

Rest

Kerri placed her little leaves
together and smiled.
"Namaste, friends,"
she whispered gently.

Affirmation:
"I honor the
light in me."

Namaste

How to Use This Book

This book invites children to move, breathe, and relax with the friends in the Garden of H.O.P.E.
Each character introduces gentle yoga poses that help the body feel strong, calm, and balanced.
Children can follow along at their own pace — there is no need to rush.
You can read the story first, then try the poses together, or pause after each pose and practice before turning the page.

Here are a few simple tips:

Move slowly. Yoga is about gentle movement, not perfection.

Breathe deeply. Take slow breaths in and out during each pose.

Listen to your body. If something feels uncomfortable, take a rest.

Have fun together. Yoga is even better when practiced with friends.

At the end of the book, the friends practice Garden Breathing and Garden Rest, helping everyone relax after their yoga adventure. Remember to rest.

Acknowledgments

With heartfelt gratitude to my husband, John, for his unwavering love and support throughout every step of this journey.

To my family, friends, and everyone who has encouraged The Dandelion Friends to grow, thank you for believing in the power of stories, kindness, and hope.

Special thanks to the children, parents, educators, counselors, and caregivers who inspire these books and remind us that even the smallest moments of peace can make a big difference.

And to Kerri, the little dandelion who began it all—thank you for gently reminding us to slow down, breathe deeply, and find calm within our hearts.

For Kevin & Jamie,
I love you both with all my heart.
May your hearts always know peace.

From the Author

Yoga and mindfulness can help children slow down, stretch their bodies, and notice their feelings in gentle ways.

In this garden, the Dandelion Friends practice breathing, movement, rest, and kindness together.

As you read this book, remember:

There is no “perfect” way to do yoga.

Children may wobble, giggle, pause, or rest.

The goal is not perfection — it is connection, calm, and confidence.

You can encourage children to:

Take slow breaths.

Move at their own pace.

Listen to their bodies.

Notice how each pose makes them feel.

Most importantly, remind them that they are safe, loved, and enough exactly as they are.

May this book bring peaceful moments to your home, classroom, or garden.

With love,

Lisa Bolton

The Dandelion Project

Explore The Dandelion Friends

Join Kerri and her friends as they discover hope, friendship, comfort, and courage through their adventures in the garden.

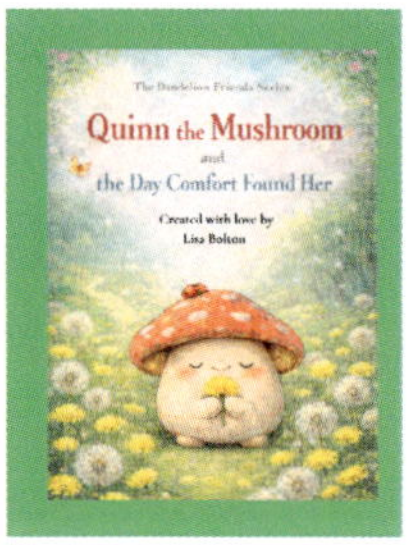

More Adventures to Come

The wind has always been Kerri's friend. One day, it carries her far beyond the garden she calls home, across forests, meadows, oceans, ponds, farms, mountains, deserts, and places she has never seen before. As she travels, Kerri meets new friends wherever the wind takes her. Some are brave, some are shy, some are worried, and some are still discovering who they are. Together, they share adventures, learn about the world around them, and discover that kindness, courage, hope, and friendship can bloom anywhere. With every journey, Kerri learns something new and helps others find the strength and beauty already growing inside their hearts. Where will the wind carry her next?

Coming Soon

The Dandelion Friends and the Day the North Star Came to the Garden

A heartwarming holiday story celebrating kindness, friendship, and the joy of giving.

Faith in the Garden Collection

Faith-based adventures inspired by hope, love, and God's promises.

The Dandelion Friends Educator Kit

Story-based curriculum, printable resources, mindfulness activities, and classroom materials inspired by The Dandelion Friends.

Made in the USA
Coppell, TX
27 June 2026

83631013R00026